Real Size Science

Plants

Rebecca Rissman

Raintree is an imprint of Capstone Global Library Limited, a company incorporated in England and Wales having its registered office at 7 Pilgrim Street, London, EC4V 6LB – Registered company number: 6695582

www.raintreepublishers.co.uk
myorders@raintreepublishers.co.uk

Text © Capstone Global Library Limited 2014
First published in hardback in 2014
The moral rights of the proprietor have been asserted.

Edited by Rebecca Rissman, Daniel Nunn, and John-Paul Wilkins
Designed by Joanna Malivoire and Tim Bond
Picture research by Ruth Blair
Production by Sophia Argyris
Originated by Capstone Global Library Ltd
Printed and bound in China by South China Printing Company

ISBN 978 1 406 26350 3
17 16 15 14 13
10 9 8 7 6 5 4 3 2 1

British Library Cataloguing in Publication Data
Rissman, Rebecca.
Plants. – (Real size science)
571.3'2-dc23
A full catalogue record for this book is available from the British Library.

Acknowledgements
We would like to thank the following for permission to reproduce photographs: Getty Images p. 17 (GAP Photos); Shutterstock pp. 4 (© Richard Griffin), 5 (© jmarkow), 6 (© Adchariyaphoto), 7 (© f9photos), 8 (© Svetlana Kuznetsova), 9 main (© Vaclav Mach) 9 inset (© mikfoto), 10 (© Kim Doucette), 11 (© Dirk Ercken), 12 main (© mikenorton), 12 inset (© Joao Virissimo), 13 (© Beneda Miroslav), 14 (© Mazzzur), 15 (© MC_PP), 16 (© Tatiana Grozetskaya), 18 (© Marie C Fields), 19 main (© sayhmog), 19 inset (© kzww), 20 (© Melinda Fawver), 21 (© Porojnicu Stelian), 22 rose (© LanKS), 22 miniature rose (© Richard Griffin).

Cover photograph of daisies in a field reproduced with permission of Shutterstock (© aleks.k).

We would like to thank Dee Reid and Nancy Harris for their invaluable help in the preparation of this book.

Every effort has been made to contact copyright holders of material reproduced in this book. Any omissions will be rectified in subsequent printings if notice is given to the publisher.

Contents

Plant parts

Plants have different parts.

Each part helps the plant to grow.

Roots

Most plants grow roots into soil.

root

Roots hold plants in place.
Roots take in nutrients.

Radishes are roots you can eat.
Radishes are a healthy snack!

Real size

Real Size

A crocus is a
small plant.
Its roots are
very thin.

Stems

Stems hold plants up.

stem →

Real Size

Stems carry nutrients from the roots to the rest of the plant.

11

Cactuses can be large plants.

This cactus stem is covered in spines.

Real size

Dill stems are very thin.

Dill is a popular herb to eat!

Leaves

Leaves take in energy from the Sun.

Real size

Leaves make energy for the rest of the plant.

Real Size

Maple trees are large plants.
Their leaves turn red and fall
off the tree in autumn.

Baby tears plants grow many small leaves. Their leaves are so small they are hard to see!

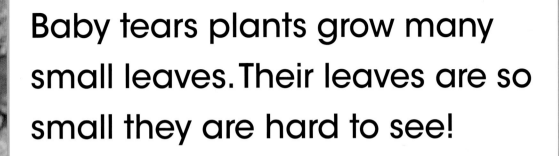

Real size

Flowers

Flowers contain pollen.

pollen

seed

Real size

Flowers can grow seeds
for more plants.

19

Peony plants have large flowers.
They are beautiful colours.

Real Size

Edelweiss plants have small flowers.
They grow on tall mountains.

Real size surprise!

Roses can be different sizes!

Picture glossary

herb type of plant used to flavour foods

nutrient something in food that living things need to grow

pollen fine yellow powder made by flowers

Index

Notes for parents and teachers

Before reading

- Engage children in a discussion about plant sizes. Ask children to think of different ways we describe size, such as tall, short, wide, or thin.
- Tell children that we can use tools, such as rulers, to measure size. We can also use body parts, such as hand lengths and foot lengths, to measure size.

After reading

- Tell children that plant parts can be many different sizes. Ask children to compare the leaves on page 14 with the maple leaf on page 16. Which is larger? Encourage children to measure the leaves with a ruler.
- Using their hand as a measurement tool, have children compare the flowers on pages 20–21. How big is the peony (e.g., one hand width), and how big is the edelweiss flower (e.g., two finger widths).